T0083170

Anthems
for SA & Men

9 anthems for sopranos,
altos, and unison men

MUSIC DEPARTMENT

OXFORD
UNIVERSITY PRESS

OXFORD
UNIVERSITY PRESS

Great Clarendon Street, Oxford OX2 6DP,
United Kingdom

Oxford University Press is a department of the University of Oxford.
It furthers the University's objective of excellence in research, scholarship,
and education by publishing worldwide. Oxford is a registered trade mark of
Oxford University Press in the UK and in certain other countries

This collection © Oxford University Press 2018

Each composer has asserted his/her right under the Copyright, Designs and
Patents Act, 1988, to be identified as the Composer of their Work(s)

Database right Oxford University Press (maker)

First published 2018

Impression: 3

All rights reserved. No part of this publication may be reproduced,
stored in a retrieval system, or transmitted, in any form or by any means,
without the prior permission in writing of Oxford University Press

Permission to perform the works in this anthology in public
(except in the course of divine worship) should normally be obtained
from the Performing Right Society Ltd (PRS) at www.prsformusic.com
or a local performing right licensing organization, unless the owner or the
occupier of the premises being used already holds a licence from such an
organization. Likewise, permission to make and exploit a recording must
be obtained in advance from the Mechanical-Copyright Protection
Society Ltd (MCPS) at www.prsformusic.com or a local mechanical
copyright licensing organization

Enquiries concerning reproduction outside the scope of the above should be
directed to the Music Rights Department, Oxford University Press, at
music.permissions.uk@oup.com or at the address above

ISBN 978-0-19-352417-0

Music and text origination by
Katie Johnston
Printed in Great Britain on acid-free paper by
Halstan & Co. Ltd, Amersham, Bucks.

Contents

Alleluia, sing to Jesus! 5
Alan Smith

Bless to me this day 12
Cecilia McDowall

Faith, hope, and love remain 24
Malcolm Archer

Fill your hearts with joy and gladness 31
Sarah Quartel

From the break of the day 35
Alan Bullard

I lift my eyes 42
Bob Chilcott

O God, you speak your beauty every hour 53
Howard Helvey

Praise the Lord, ye heavens adore him 61
Alan Bullard

This day 67
Bob Chilcott

Alleluia, sing to Jesus!

William Chatterton Dix (adap.)
(1837–98)

ALAN SMITH
(1962–2017)

Duration: 3 mins

Also published separately in a version for SATB and organ (ISBN 978–0–19–339568–8). This version has been prepared by Alan Bullard.

© Oxford University Press 2013 and 2018. Photocopying this copyright material is ILLEGAL.

13
Hark, the songs of peace-ful Si - on Thun-der like a might - y flood;
Man.
17
Je - sus, out of ev - 'ry na - tion, has re - deemed us by his
Ped.
21
blood.
mp
Al-le-
mf
sim.
Man.

25
-lu - ia, not as or - phans Are we left in sor - row now, Al-le-
mp
Ped.
29
-lu - ia, he is near us, Faith be-lieves, nor ques - tions how:
3
33
mf
Though the cloud from sight re-ceived him When the for - ty days were o'er,
mf
Man.

37
Shall our hearts for - get his pro - mise, 'I am with you ev - er -
mf
mp
Ped.
Man.
41
p
-more'?
p
più legato
45
mp
Al - le - lu - ia, bread of an - gels, Here on earth our food and stay;

49
mp
Al - le - lu - ia, here the sin - ful Flee to you from day to day.
53
In - ter - ces - sor, friend of sin - ners, Earth's Re - deem - er, plead for me,
all the sin - less Sweep a-cross the cry - stal
57
Where the songs of all the sin - less Sweep a - cross the cry - stal

61
unis. f
sea.
Al-le - lu - ia, King e- ter - nal The
f
f
Ped.
65
Lord of lords we own;
Al-le - lu - ia, born of Ma - ry, Earth your
sim.
69
3
3
3
foot-stool, hea-ven your throne:
You with-in the veil have en - tered, Robed in

73
flesh, our great high priest;
You on earth both priest and Sa - viour
77
In the Eu - cha - ris - - - tic feast.
82
rall.
rall.
sim.
ff

Bless to me this day

St Brendan the Voyager (484–577)
from *Carmina Gadelica*, Vol. III (1940)

CECILIA McDOWALL
(b. 1951)

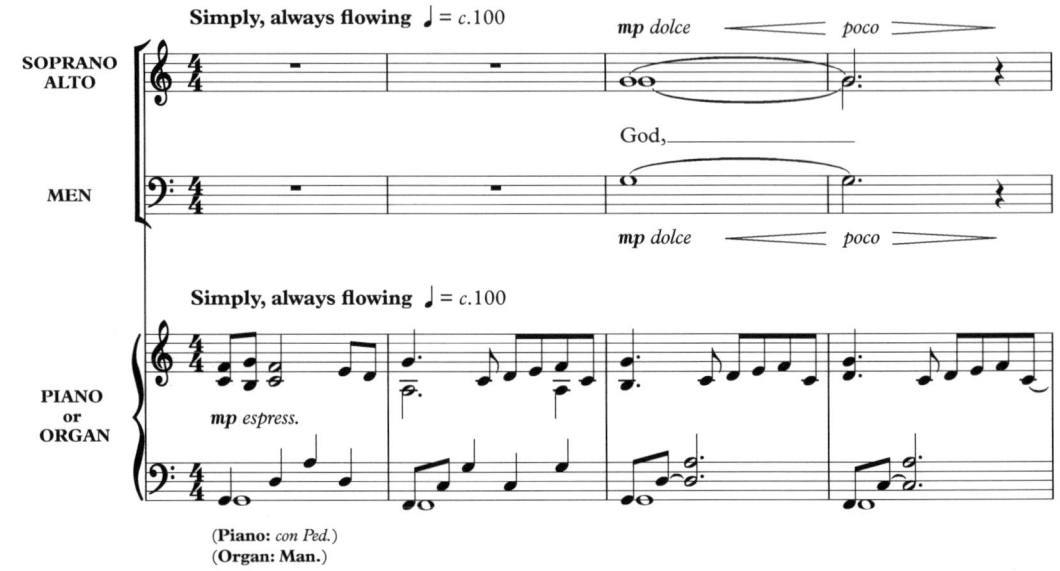

Duration: 4 mins

Also published separately in a version for SA and piano/organ (ISBN 978–0–19–338621–1).

© Oxford University Press 2016 and 2018. Photocopying this copyright material is ILLEGAL.

9
mp
mf
bless this day, bless this day,
mp
mf
mp
mf
(Ped.)
13
p
mp
God, bless to me, bless
p
mp
p
mp
bless this
f
17
mf
this night, bless this
mf
f
mf
f

pochiss. rit.
20
S.
night, this night; Bless, O
mf
A.
night, this night; Bless, O
mf
M.
night, this night;
pochiss. rit.
24
a tempo
bless, thou God of grace,
bless, O bless, thou God of grace, of grace, thou God of
mf
Bless, O bless, thou God of grace,
a tempo
mf
(Man.)

28
f
Each day and hour of my life, of life.
f
grace, Each hour of my life, of my life.
f
Each day and hour of my life, of life.
f
32
mp
mf
O bless, O bless, thou God,
mp
mf
O bless, O bless, thou God, thou God of grace,
mp
mf
Bless, thou God, thou God of grace,
mp
mf

36
mp
mf
Each day and hour of my life.
Each day and hour of my life, of my life.
Each day and hour of my life, of my life.
mp
mf
f legato
41
mp
poco
mp
God, bless the
God, bless the
God, bless the

* Small notes indicate optional *divisi*.

54
p
mp
God, bless the earth that is be-
mp
bless the earth, bless the earth be-
p
mp
God, bless the earth, the earth that is be-
mp
(Man.)
57
mf
f
-neath my sole, God, bless the earth, the
mf
f
-neath my sole, God, bless the earth, the
mf
f
-neath my sole, God, bless the earth, the
mf
f

61
mf
pochiss. rit. a tempo
earth; Bless, O God,
mf
earth; Bless, O God,
mf
earth; Bless, O God,
pochiss. rit. a tempo
mf
(Ped.)
65
and give to me thy love, O God of
and give to me thy love, give to me thy love, Of
and give to me thy love, O God of

69
f
mp
gods, bless my rest and my re-pose; O bless, O
gods, bless my rest; O bless, O
gods, bless my rest and my re-pose;
(Man.)

73
mf
mp
God, O bless, bless my
God, and give to me thy love, bless my
God, and give to me thy love, bless my

77
mf
f
pochiss. rit.
rest, my re - pose. Bless, O
rest, my re - pose, my re - pose. Bless, O
rest, my re - pose, my re - pose.
pochiss. rit.
(Ped.)
81
a tempo
God, and give to me thy love,
God, and give to me thy love, give to me thy
God, and give to me thy love,
a tempo
(Ped.)

85
O God of gods, bless my rest and my re-pose,
love, Of gods, bless my rest,
O God of gods, bless my rest and my re-pose,
89
mf
And bless, O God,
mp
and bless, O God,
mf
And bless, O God of gods,
mp
and bless, O God of gods,
mf
And bless, O God,
mp
and bless, O God,
mf
mp

93
dim. poco a poco
and bless, O God, my re - pose,
dim. poco a poco
and bless, O God of gods, my re - pose,
dim. poco a poco
and bless, O God, my re - pose,
dim. poco a poco
ritardando
97
pp
my re - pose, re - pose.
pp
my re - pose.
pp
my re - pose, re - pose.
ritardando
pp

Faith, hope, and love remain

1 Corinthians 13: 13 and Song of Solomon 8: 6–7

MALCOLM ARCHER
(b. 1952)

Duration: 4 mins

Also published in versions for SATB and organ (ISBN 978–0–19–338924–3), and SA and organ/piano (ISBN 978–0–19–340165–5).

© Oxford University Press 2012 and 2018. Photocopying this copyright material is ILLEGAL.

12
faith, hope, and love, faith, hope, and
(Man.)
15
cresc.
mf
love, but the great - est of these is love, but the
cresc.
(Ped.)
18
great - est of these is love.
mf
21
M.
MEN mf
And now these three re - main:

24
faith, hope, and love, faith, hope, and
27
f
mf
love, but the great - est of these is love, but the
30
S.
A.
M.
For
S.
mf
A.
mf For love is strong as
mf
great - est of these is love. For

33
death, is strong as death, strong as
36
f
death, strong as death. Ma - ny
f
39
mf
mp
wa - ters can - not quench love, nei - ther can the floods
mf
mp

43
p
drown it, drown it.
p
mp
47
poco rall.
a tempo
mp
And now these three re-main:
mp
poco rall.
a tempo
51
faith, hope, and love, faith, hope, and

54
mf
f
love, but the great - est of these is love, but the
mf
f
f
57
ff
f
these
great - est of is love, is
these, the great - est of these ff f
(Tuba)
ff
60
mf
poco rall.
love, but the great - est of these is
mf
poco rall.
f
mf

63
a tempo
mp
love.
mp
a tempo
mp
(Man.)
66
70
rall.
rall.
p
(Ped.)

Fill your hearts with joy and gladness

Timothy Dudley-Smith
(b. 1926)

SARAH QUARTEL
(b. 1982)

Duration: *c.*2 mins

Also published in a version for flexible voices in *The Oxford Book of Easy Flexible Anthems* (ISBN 978–0–19–341325–2).

Music © Oxford University Press 2017 and 2018. Text © Timothy Dudley-Smith in Europe and Africa; © Hope Publishing Company in the United States of America and the rest of the world. Reproduced by permission of Oxford University Press. All rights reserved. Photocopying this copyright material is ILLEGAL.

* The keyboard part may be omitted in verse 3, entering in bar 29.

25
mf
grass up-on the moun-tain pas-tures, gold-en val - leys thick with grain.
mf
mf
tenuto
a tempo
29
SOPRANOS
f
4. Fill your hearts with joy and
ALTOS & MEN
f
4. Fill your hearts with joy and glad - ness,
tenuto
a tempo
mf
f
(Ped.)
32
glad - ness, with joy and glad - ness, de - clare his judg-ments,
peace and plen - ty crown your days; love his laws, de - clare his judg-ments,

36
walk in his words and ways; he the
walk in all his words and ways; he the Lord and
39
rit. al fine
ff
Lord and we his child - ren: praise the Lord, the Lord,
we his child - ren: praise the Lord, all peo - ple, praise the Lord, all peo - ple,
rit. al fine
ff
42
praise the Lord, all peo - ple, praise!
praise the Lord, all peo - ple, praise!
(Pno RH)

From the break of the day

Jan Struther
(1901–53)

ALAN BULLARD
(b. 1947)

Duration: *c.*3 mins

Also published in a version for SATB and piano/organ, available separately (ISBN 978–0–19–337141–5) and in *Alan Bullard Anthems* (ISBN 978–0–19–336931–3).

Music © Oxford University Press 2010 and 2018. Words 'Lord of all hopefulness' by Jan Struther from *Enlarged Songs of Praise*, 1931. Reproduced by permission of Oxford University Press. All rights reserved. Photocopying this copyright material is ILLEGAL.

9
cares could de - stroy.
mf
cares could de - stroy.
Be there at our wak - ing,
cares could de - stroy.
mf
mf
13
and give us, we pray, Your bliss in our hearts, Lord,
17
p
at the break of the day.
p
p

21
mf brighter
mp
faith, Whose
Lord of all ea - ger-ness, Lord of all faith,
mf brighter
mp
faith, Whose
mf brighter
mp
strong hands were skilled at the plane and the lathe,
25
mf
mf
Whose hands were skilled at the plane and the lathe,
mf
strong hands were skilled at the plane and the lathe,
mf
Be there at our la - bours and give us, we pray, Your
29
cresc.
Be there at our la - bours and give us, we pray, Your
cresc.
Be there at our la - bours, give us, we pray, Your
cresc.

strength in our
33
f
mf
strength in our hearts, Lord, at the noon of the day.
f
strength in our
mf
f
mf
37
p gently
Lord of all kind - li-ness, Lord of all
p gently
(Man.)
41
ALTOS
p gently
mp
Your hands swift to wel - come, your arms to em-
grace,
mp
mp

45
S.
mp cresc.
A.
-brace,
Be there at our hom - ing, and
cresc.
Be there at our hom - ing, and
cresc.
(Ped.)
give us, we pray, Your love in our hearts, Lord,
mf
pp
p
48
give us, we pray, Your love in our hearts, at the
mf
pp
p
give us, we pray, Your love in our hearts, at the
mf
pp
p
52
at the eve of the day.
poco rit.
eve of the day.
eve of the day.
poco rit.

Poco meno mosso ♩ = c.54
SOLO (opt.)
56
p peacefully
S.
Lord of all gen - tle-ness, Lord of all calm, Whose
p peacefully
A.
ah ah
p peacefully
M.
ah ah
Poco meno mosso ♩ = c.54
p peacefully
60
voice is con - tent - ment, whose pres - ence is balm,

64
(TUTTI)
S.
A.
M.
poco
Be there at our sleep - ing, and give us, we pray, Your
68
p
peace in our hearts, Lord, at the end of the day,
72
meno mosso
a tempo
poco rit.
pp
at the end of the day.
ppp

I lift my eyes

Timothy Dudley-Smith
(b. 1926)

BOB CHILCOTT
(b. 1955)

Duration: *c.*4 mins

Also published separately in a version for SSAA and piano (ISBN 978–0–19–337837–7).

Music © Oxford University Press 2011 and 2018. Text © Timothy Dudley-Smith in Europe and Africa; © Hope Publishing Company in the United States of America and the rest of the world. Reproduced by permission of Oxford University Press. All rights reserved. Photocopying this copyright material is ILLEGAL.

10
p
S.
ah
I
A.
lift my eyes, I lift my eyes, I lift my eyes. I
M.
lift my eyes, I lift my eyes, I lift my eyes.
13
unis.
S./A.
lift my eyes to the qui - et hills in the press of a bu - sy day; as
15
green hills stand in a dust - y land so God is my strength and stay.

17
mf ma dolce
I lift my eyes, I
mf ma dolce
20
lift my eyes, I lift my eyes
23
S.
A.
p
to the qui - et hills.
p sost.

27
S./A.
unis. mp
I lift my eyes to the qui - et hills to a
M.
mp
I lift my eyes to the
mp
29
calm that is mine to share; se - cure and still in the Fa - ther's will and
qui - et hills to a calm that is mine to share; se - cure and still in the
31
S.
kept by the Fa - ther's care. I
A.
kept by the Fa - ther's care.
M.
Fa - ther's will and kept by the Fa - ther's care.

33
mf ma dolce
lift my eyes, I lift my eyes,
mf ma dolce
I lift my eyes, I lift
mf ma dolce
I lift my eyes,
mf ma dolce
36
I lift my eyes to the qui - et
my eyes, I lift my eyes to the qui - et
I lift my eyes to the qui - et

39
S.
A.
M.
mp
mf
hills.
I lift my eyes to the qui-
42
- et hills with a prayer as I turn to sleep; by
45
day, by night, through the dark and light my

47
Shep-herd will guard his sheep.
50
S./A.
S./A. unis. p
I
p sost.
54
lift my eyes to the qui - et hills and my heart to the Fa - ther's throne; in
56
all my ways to the end of days the Lord will pre-serve his own.

58
mf ma dolce
I lift my eyes, I
mf ma dolce
61
lift my eyes, I lift my eyes
64
S.
A.
to the qui - et hills.
I

67
f
S.
lift my eyes, I lift my eyes,
f
A.
I lift my eyes, I lift
f
M.
I lift my eyes,
f
70
I lift my eyes to the qui - et
my eyes, I lift my eyes to the qui - et
I lift my eyes to the qui - et

73
p
hills.
p
hills.
p
hills.
p sost.
77
ALTOS p
A.
Lift my eyes, lift my eyes, I lift my eyes,
80
S.
p
ah
A.
I lift my eyes.
Lift my eyes, lift my eyes,
M.
p
Lift my eyes, lift my eyes, I

83
pp
I lift my eyes, I lift my eyes.
Lift my eyes,
lift my eyes, I lift my eyes.
Lift my eyes,
pp
pp
86
pp
rit.
ah
I lift my eyes.
lift my eyes, I lift my eyes, I lift my eyes.
lift my eyes, I lift my eyes, I lift my eyes.
rit.

O God, you speak your beauty every hour

Words and music by
HOWARD HELVEY
'MARCUM'

Duration: *c.*4 mins

Also published separately in a version for SATB and organ (ISBN 978–0–19–341273–6).

© Oxford University Press 2015 and 2018. Photocopying this copyright material is ILLEGAL.

9
mp
O God, you speak your beau - ty ev - 'ry
13
S./A. unis. mp
In
hour, from soar - ing peaks to val - leys fed by springs.
17
ev - 'ry liv - ing soul and fra - grant flow'r your han - di -

21
mf
-work is seen cre - a - tion sings!
As peo - ple in your
mf
mf
25
unis.
im - age, we a - spire and live to mir - ror your cre -
3
3
3
29
mp
-a - tive fire.
mp
mp (reduce)

* If necessary, the organ may lightly double the choral parts from b. 37 to b. 55.

45
hand we move from depths be - low to heights a -
49
mp
grace ex -
-bove. May we, with hearts up - lift - ed by your grace, ex -
mp
53
-tend your
mf
-tend your love to ev - 'ry land and race.
mf
mf
(Man.)
mf
Ped.
57
3
3
(add)

62
poco rit.
cresc.
poco meno mosso ♩ = c.96
66
SOPRANOS
f
O Spi - rit, giv - ing breath to all the earth, we
ALTOS & MEN
f
O Spi - rit, giv - ing breath to all the earth, we
poco meno mosso ♩ = c.96
f
70
grow in faith and strength from your clear flame. O Wind of Heav'n, re-
grow in faith and strength from your clear flame. O Wind of Heav'n, re -

74
-called at our re - birth, the world a-waits the u -
-called at our re - birth, the world a - waits the
78
- ni - ty we claim. With zeal we strive, as - sist - ed by your
u - ni - ty we claim. With zeal we strive, as - sist - ed by your
82
poco rit.
might, to fill the earth with ev - er - last - ing
might, to fill the earth with ev - er - last - ing
poco rit.

86
a tempo
poco rit.
Light.
Light.
a tempo
poco rit.
poco meno mosso ♩ = c.92
90
S.
A.
M.
più f
We'll fill the earth with ev - er - last -
più f
poco meno mosso ♩ = c.92
più f
allargando
94
- ing Light.
allargando

Praise the Lord, ye heavens adore him

Anon., from *Foundling Hospital Collection*, 1796/1801 (altd)
Based on Psalm 148: 1–6, 14

ALAN BULLARD
(b. 1947)

Duration: *c.*2 mins

Also published separately in a version for SATB and organ/piano (ISBN 978–0–19–339567–1).

© Oxford University Press 2013 and 2018. Photocopying this copyright material is ILLEGAL.

13
Lord, for he hath spo - ken; Worlds his might - y voice o - beyed; And
17
laws, that ne - ver shall be bro - ken, For their guid - ance he hath
21
made.

25
p legato
Praise him, an - gels in the
mp
Praise the Lord, ye heav'ns a - dore him; Praise him, an - gels in the
p
29
height; Praise him, all ye stars and
height; Sun and moon, bow down be - fore him, Praise him, all ye stars and
33
mf
light. Praise the Lord, for he is glo - rious; Ne - ver shall his pro-mise
mf
light. Praise the Lord, praise the
mf

* small notes optional

50
an - gels in the height; Sun and moon, bow down be - fore him, Praise him,
54
ff
all ye stars and light. Praise the God of our sal - va - tion; An - gel
ff
all ye stars, praise him, all ye stars and light. Praise the God of our sal
ff
58
hosts his pow'r pro - claim; For heav'n and earth, and all cre - a - tion,
-va - tion; An - gel hosts his pow'r pro - claim; For heav'n and earth, and

* optional Soprano *divisi*

This day

Jewish text
adap. Bob Chilcott

BOB CHILCOTT
(b. 1955)

Duration: *c.*2 mins

Also published in a version for SA and piano as part of the larger work, *This Day* (ISBN 978–0–19–335933–8).

© Oxford University Press 2007 and 2018. Photocopying this copyright material is ILLEGAL.

7
mf
This day in-scribe us for a hap - py, hap - py life.
mf
mf
10
mp
This day hear our cry.
mf
This day, this
mp
mf
This day ac - cept our prayer in
mp
mf
13
day.
This day, this day.
mer - cy and fa-vour.
This day sup-port us with your right - eous hand.

This day ac-cept our prayer in mer - cy and fa-vour.
16
f
mf
This day, this day. This day, this
f
mf
f
mf
19
mp
dolce
day.
This day, this
dolce
mp
This day will you strength us.
mp dolce
22
day. This day, this day.
This day will you bless us. This day will you lift us, vi - sit us for good.

25
mf
This day in-scribe us for a hap - py, hap - py, life.
mf
mf
28
mp
espress.
S.
This day hear our cry.
A - men, a -
mp
espress.
A.
This day hear our cry.
A -
mp
espress.
M.
This day hear our cry.
A - men,
mp
espress.

31
mf
-men, a - men, a - men, a -
mf
- men, a - men, a - men, a -
mf
a - men, a - men, a - men, a -
mf
35
dim.
p
- men, a - men.
dim.
p
- men, a - men.
dim.
p
- men, a - men.
poco rit.
a bit slower
rit.
dim.
p